HOW TO SAVE YOUR HOME FROM FORECLOSURE AND SAVE THOUSANDS OF DOLLARS

Don't Lose Your Dream

Geoffrey G. Hawthorne

Outskirts Press, Inc.
Denver, Colorado

Outskirts Press, Inc.
http://www.outskirtspress.com

ISBN: 978-1-4327-3764-1

Outskirts Press and the "OP" logo are trademarks belonging to Outskirts Press, Inc.

PRINTED IN THE UNITED STATES OF AMERICA

About The Author

My name is Geoffrey G. Hawthorne. I owned Hawthorne Associates Auditing Business for over twenty years and I am still an active member of various accounting associations. I decided to go into the mortgage business as a mortgage executive with a local savings bank for over four years in the nineteen eighties. Having liked the business, I decided to open my own, Hawthorne Associates, licensed with the NYS Banking Department in August, nineteen eighty nine. As a mortgage broker, having both an accounting and mortgage background, I can safely say that I have never had a complaint from a client.

I have never had a NYS Banking Department complaint or fine since operations began. I can safely say that I have never given a client a mortgage at the so-called one percent and above negative amortization loans. These loans that adjust monthly with mortgage loan caps up to seventeen percent on the life of the loans. I refuse to give a client one of those loans, explaining the consequences. I have had the same clients go to other brokers, bankers and banks to obtain the same loans without explaining how the loans work.

About Loans

On a majority of the above loans, you apply through mail and the lender mails you the forms to sign. After the lender takes your information over the telephone and after signing the loan documents, in most states, the lender will set up an appointment at your home. Usually, the lender will have a Title Company present to notarize the loan document. It is not for the Title Company to explain the loan to the borrower. It is the lender's job to explain the loan. The representatives are at the closing to go over the title charges, not to explain bank and points charged to the borrower.

Many borrowers have taken the loan and found later that the lender did not explain the mortgage received, after closing, to them. This is partly to blame on the borrower and lender alike. If the borrower would have gone to their attorney or accountant and paid a small consultation fee for advice on how the loan worked, I am sure the foreclosures now and in the future would not have happened.

I personally expect to see over three million borrowers go into foreclosure and lose their homes due to deceptive loans given out by some brokers, bankers, Real Estates, Builders, etc. to make a fast dollar. As I am writing this book, I foresee the mortgage crisis only getting worse, as this is only the tip of the iceberg.

Deceived

In some states there is a mortgage tax, let's take the NYS mortgage tax as an example. NYS charges a mortgage tax in the five boroughs of New York City of 2.03 % on every mortgage. This is regardless whether or not the mortgage is a purchase or a refinance, on one to four family homes or condominiums, *not* the co-ops.

This tax is paid as follows; the borrower pays 1.78% and the lender pays .25% as an example. A loan of $150,000 equals a charge to the borrower of $150,000 x 1.78%= $2,670.00. The lender pays $150,000 x .25%= $375.00.

There is a total mortgage tax paid to NYS of 3,045.00 every time a borrower purchases or refinances a home or condominium. In the five boroughs, if there is up to a $500,000 mortgage, then the percentage increases. In other areas of NYS the mortgage tax decreases by county.

Savings

The way to save thousands on NYS or other States where there is a mortgage tax on refinances only, let's take the five boroughs. It goes as follows:

The mortgage tax is 2.03%. For instance, we will take the $150,000 mortgages. You take a refinance out for $225,000. You originally owed $150,000; therefore you are taking additional $75,000 cash out for home improvements or debts, etc. When refinancing you would first shop for the lowest rate, then tell the lender or the bank, which has the original mortgage that you want to save the mortgage tax on the original mortgage of $150,000.

This is called a *CEMA,* which is a Consolidation Extension and Modification Agreement. Whereas you will save the $2,670.00 on the closing of your new mortgage and only pay for what is called New Money, which is the $75,000 extra you are borrowing. This is 1.78 x 75,000= 1,335.00 instead of 1.78 on the total of $225,000 x 1.78= 4005.00, which is a savings of $2,

670.00 on your closing, as the refinanced loan amount on old money is saved.

For the borrowers who have refinanced over the past two years, to find out if you paid only on the new money, not the old money, look at the Settlement Statement. This is also called the U.S Department of Housing and Urban Development or also called a HUD-1. This gives you an itemized statement of closing costs, which by law, you must get a copy of the statement when you close.

If you paid the mortgage tax for the full amount of the refinance instead of only the new money, then I suggest going to the broker, banker or bank and ask why you had to pay mortgage tax on the total, instead of the New Money only.

When refinancing with a Bank Attorney there is a charge for the CEMA, as you are signing *two* mortgage loans into one new mortgage. You are signing for the old money and the new money.

Title Savings

When refinancing, you originally had to have a Title Search when you purchased your home. When you apply for your refinance always tell the broker, banker, or bank that you want a Title Discount. This is called a Re-Issue. It is necessary to bring your original HUD-1 Settlement Statement with you.

If you usually closed your original loan on a purchase or refinance in the past two years you can save hundreds of dollars on the Title Charges on a Re-Issue Rate. Title Charges are based on the amount of the mortgage. Ask your attorney who originally ordered the Title for you for a copy if you misplaced yours. You must also bring your loan papers to your attorney for review. Have them explain the new loan you are taking or go to your accountant for a review of the documents given to you before setting up a closing.

How To Apply For A New Mortgage Or A Refinance

If refinancing for a lower rate, try to review the new loan with either an attorney or accountant. I would review the original loan with my client, if the client just wants to lower his monthly payment, it is called a Rate and Term Refinance.

Let's take a mortgage amount of $200,000. My client now pays $1398.00 principle interest on a thirty year fixed rate mortgage. He has had his mortgage two years, the current thirty year fixed rate is 6 ½ %, and he is now paying 7 ½ %. Figuring his new mortgage at 6 ½ %, his new payment on $200,000 and closing costs saving on mortgage tax and the Title Re-Issue Rate, his closing costs will be approximately $5,500 in NYS. Saving 2 ¼ % and using 2 ¾ % = 5 % closing costs. Closing costs would normally be 5% minimum, in NYS which would be $10,000 in closing costs. That means it would cost my borrower $1329.00 principle and interest. As he would either add the closing cost to the $200,000 making the loan $210,000 and paying $1329.30 per month, or my borrower paying the $10,000 closing cost out of pocket. This would then cost him $1266.00 per month. The difference is a savings of $132.00 per month, costing my client $10,000 in out of pocket closing costs at 5%= $10,000, by using the savings of CEMA and Title, his closing cost would be $5,500 in NY, out of pocket.

In order to refinance, I would recommend a difference of at least 2% decrease in rate or *do not* refinance. On the first example, by saving $132.00 per month, it would take six years and four months to make up the cost to refinance. Since it just cost you $10,000 in closing cost, seventy-six months at $132.00 savings per month equals $10,032.00. Usually, most borrowers stay in their homes for seven years. Using the above principle, it does not pay in this case to refinance unless you have a 7 ½ % adjustable rate, which goes higher, then refinance to a fixed rate.

How To Refinance Adjustable And Sub-Prime Mortgages

First, do not go back to the broker, banker or lender who gave you the loan, as they are out to do it all over again.

Have you noticed in some advertisements that the same lenders that gave out the monthly 1% and above Negative Amortization Loans with maximum caps, some at 17% are now offering you fixed rates and FHA Loans to get you back in? Ask yourself, why did they give you monthly loans in the first place? If you qualified for a Fixed Rate Loan, answer is making more money on you over and over again. Once again look at the Foreclosure Percent, which is only going to get worse.

Common sense would tell you if you're taking the rate at 2% monthly and the fixed rate is 6%, why would a lender lose the 4%? He is not giving you a gift. The 4% they're not getting is added to your original loan every month and is going up. This means as the lenders rates go up to your 17%, it is all added to your original mortgage. This is called Negative Amortization.

Think about what is happening to your mortgage. If you had a $200,000 mortgage, eventually you would probably wind up owing $250,000 to $300,000. This means you paid $250,000 for your home and put $50,000 down. You will wind up forking over $250,000. Think about it for a minute.

How To Get Out Of It

First check your credit score, most banks and lenders use a Tri-Merge Credit report. This report will show your three scores. The first score is called, Equifax Beacon Scores, the second is called an Experian FICO Score, and the third is called a Trans-Union FICO Score, which you can obtain by either going online or calling to order your credit reports. There is a small cost on each for adding your score to the credit report.

Below is the contact information for each company. First call each company, they will instruct you on how to obtain each, either online by Internet or by mail. Remember that you need the scores. The contacts are as follows:

EFX- EQUIFAX INFORMATION SVCS
P.O. Box 740241, Atlanta, GA 30374
Phone: (800) 685-1111

XPN- EXPERIAN
P.O. Box 2002, Allen, TX 75013
Phone: (888) 397-3742

TUC- TRANS UNION
P.O Box 34012, Fullerton, CA 92834

The minimum middle score must be a 620 FICO Score to start you on obtaining a Conforming Fixed Mortgage, a Conforming Fixed Rate Mortgage is what we call, 'A' Paper. Which means, your rate is much lower as your middle score on your credit report is the minimum of 620 or higher and you can verify enough income to qualify for a Conforming Fixed Rate Mortgage.

I would also like to point out on your Credit Report, if you have judgments, tax liens from State and Federal or open collection accounts, they must be paid and shown as satisfied before applying. I suggest a letter of explanation as to why you had same, when applying for a Conventional Fixed Rate Mortgage.

Below is a list of the maximum mortgage amounts to obtain "A" Conforming Fixed rate mortgage, if your mortgage is over the maximum amount, you will have to get a Non-Conforming Mortgage or Conventional Non-Conforming Mortgage. The fixed rates are much higher, as you are borrowing much more money.

Remember the limits below on numbers 1, 2, 3, and 4 will be increasing in the near future.

Number Of Units	Conforming Loan Amounts for Continental U.S.	New Conforming Loan Amounts for Alaska, Hawaii and U.S. Virgin Islands
1	$417,000.00	$625,500.00
2	$533,850.00	$800,775.00
3	$645,300.00	$967,950.00
4	$801,950.00	$1,202,925.00

I know the majority of people who go bankrupt had no choice, due to the loss of a job, divorce, or they did not realize they were overextended on credit cards and could not pay them. Years ago if someone went bankrupt, they would be ashamed that they got into that situation and would not let family, friends, etc. know their circumstances. Today, some people go bankrupt, sometimes twice in their life for no other reason than that they know the system and charge up a storm, knowing they won't have to pay, and then brag about what they did.

Through the years of seeing these bankruptcies, I know some have no shame as to what they did. I would like to mention that I have known many people that have gotten in trouble with credit charges, mortgages, etc. and the same people will take an extra job to pay off their debts or do a cash-out Refinance to pay their debts, as the same people have what is called, pride, and know that they will someday obtain a good credit rating the hard way.

Unfortunately these same people will be ruined for at least six to ten years with poor credit and must go to Sub Prime, sometimes Predatory Lending with much higher rates and mortgages, because they refuse to walk away from their debts. Again, I have known some people that could care less and charge up a storm and always go bankrupt.

Now the lending institutions' guidelines are that you could have gone bankrupt over two years ago, owing thousands of dollars and walked away from debt and obtain a discharge of the same debt through the courts and established new credit for over two years and get your credit score above the 620 FICO score and applied for a Conforming Fixed Rate Mortgage with 'A' Paper rates, when the poor guy who had too much pride by trying to pay his debts must go for a much higher interest rate on *his* mortgage.

Figure this one out. It does not make any sense.

Here is another scenario. If you are a person who always paid your bills and never had credit, always paid by cash, you are considered, 'No credit is bad credit.' The only way to get a mortgage is with documented rent receipts, letters from your landlords, utility bills, cable bills, etc. in your name or car insurance.

I suggest obtaining a letter from each, to verify that you pay your bills on time. Once again, the 620 FICO Middle Score is not the only item the lender will review. It is how much total debt and monthly total payments are shown on your credit, as you must have a sufficient amount of income to cover both your monthly debt and the mortgage added to the debt to qualify.

Since you cannot write off interest on your

debt, I suggest reviewing your credit card statements and start more on the cards showing the most interest and less on the credit cards showing the lower interest. Once you payoff a high interest card, then go to the next one. Try calling up each creditor and negotiate the total amount owed at a discount. Another way is to gather all your bills and find out if it is feasible to take a Home Equity Loan out at a fixed rate at Prime, which is now at 5.000% or you can take a Cash out Refinance on your residence at currently 6.500% and payoff your credit cards, which run about 10% for a short period of time, then increase. With cards that have interest rates up to 29.9%, you will also be able to take a write-off on your mortgage interest at the end of the year. By following this procedure you could save hundreds of dollars or more by comparing one new monthly mortgage payment with no other monthly debt. Compared to your current monthly debt and mortgage from your triMerge Credit Report, I guarantee you will save hundreds of dollars per month.

For example, let's say your credit Report is over the 620 Middle Score, below shows your total debt owed.

XYZ Bank	Balance Owed	Monthly Payment	Interest Charged
XYZ Bank MTGE.	**$250,000**	**$1,940**	**7%**
Sears	$2,500	$130.00	25.99%
Macys	$1,750	$100.00	26.99%
XYZ Bank	$7,000	$250.00	24.99%
Misc./Others	$15,000	$400.00	16.99%
Totals	$276,250	$2820.00	

By refinancing Cash Out, you apply for $282,000.00 to cover the closing costs at 6.500% thirty year Fixed, your new monthly mortgage would be:

Mtge: $1,785.00   Per month
             $ 200.00 Taxes
             $ 75.00 HO Insurance.
Total: $2,060.00

Which is a monthly savings of Old: $2,820.00
New: $2,060.00
Savings: **$760.00**
per month

You now have one monthly payment of $2,060 per month, no other debt, plus saving $760.00 per month, plus the interest and property tax write off at the end of the year.

The savings could pay for your child's education, new car, improvements on your residence and many other things without touching your savings 401, IRA's, etc. You could just put the $760.00 in your savings account. This is called a Cash Out Refinance. Providing your credit is over the 620 FICO and your income is enough to qualify.

The first step is to obtain a copy of your Tri-Merge Credit Report, which will show FICO scores, total debt and total monthly payment. If you pay your own Property Tax and Homeowner Insurance, add the monthly totals to your principle and interest. Most normal banks will pay your Property Tax and Insurance for you; otherwise, add this to your monthly debt.

Now once you compare your actual total of all Debt, then you can compare it to a new Cash Out Fixed thirty-year mortgage. This system will take you approximately less than one hour. To figure out if it is worth your while, using the current factor, multiply 6.33 times the mortgage you will need by today's 6.500% 30-year fixed rate.

For instance you need $282,000 x 6.33 Factor =$1785.00 per month. Based on the example I have given you. Below is a factor chart for your using the Interest Rate on the day you use this system. Check with the lenders for your rate, then use the factors, or if you currently have a low fixed rate, think about Home Equity at a fixed rate to con-solidate your debts on your Credit Report.

Equal Monthly Payment Per $1000

Term Rate	15 Years	25 Years	30 Years
5%	7.91	5.85	5.37
5 1/8	7.98	5.92	5.45
5 1/4	8.04	6 %	5.53
5 3/8	8.11	6.07	5.6
5 ½	8.18	6.15	5.68
5 5/8	8.18	6.22	5.76
5 ¾	8.24	6.30	5.84
5 7/8	8.31	6.37	5.92
6%	8.38	6.45	6 %
6 1/8	8.44	6.52	6.08
6 ¼	8.51	6.60	6.16
6 3/8	8.58	6.68	6.24
6 ½	8.65	6.76	6.33
6 5/8	8.72	6.84	6.41
6 ¾	8.78	6.91	6.49
6 7/8	8.85	6.99	6.57
7 %	8.92	7.07	6.66

Over the past few years, I have received hundreds of advertisements from mortgage brokers, bankers and Banks telling me I am pre-qualified for a 1% plus mortgage and I will save hundreds of dollars per month if I call them. I have kept every one of the letters to back up my story. First let me explain how they work.

Anyone can get access to your information by just going to your County clerk's office to see if you own your own home and find out how much your mortgage is and also which bank your mortgage is with. These lenders can buy this information from various sources, including banks. This is public information at your County Clerk's office. If you ever wondered how you received this mail; that is the answer.

Telemarketer's have called me hundreds of times during dinner to ask me to refinance my mortgage. This is annoying harassment and also infringement. I am displaying a few of the ads in my book. I am positive you have seen the same ads or similar ones in your mail on the 1% and above mortgages they want you to take.

It is a pity that so many homeowners had gotten trapped into taking these loans. The same lenders, banks, brokers and bankers want to restructure the same loans. Notice the current ads and mail you will receive in the future are now trying to give you Fixed Rate loans with the same lenders, etc. Why didn't they give you the fixed rates in the first place?

(Sample of mail and Newspaper ads-I have received mail from lenders across the country, not only in NY State.)

The Sub Prime Problem and Solution
How to Get Out and Save Your Home

The worst thing that can happen to a homeowner, besides illness, is to lose their home in a foreclosure and leave them and their families homeless. How do you explain to your family that you are being left this way because you listened to a mortgage specialist? Or, how easy it was to have your dream come true, without having any money to put down? Think about what this so-called mortgage specialist told you, "Don't worry, I can get you a no money down, 100% Finance Loan, it won't cost you a dollar to get this dream for your family."

A few months later you find out that the dream has become a nightmare as your mortgage payment goes up hundreds of dollars more per month and is still going up with no end in sight. That is what the mortgage lender didn't explain as you closed the loan at your home and the title Rep could not explainThe lender told him that you are not with the borrower to explain how the mortgage payment changes, but that you are with the borrower only to notarize the documents and explain the title charges only, and maybe to explain what the borrower is being charged at closing.

If you have the HUD-1 Settlement Statement, which by law you must get a copy, then you would know item by item what is being charged. Of course the only thing you want to know at this point is, if this is for real, you will sign almost anything to own or refinance my home and get this over with. You are really at this point not interested in receiving the mortgage caps of 12 to 17% and this was not explained to you, that you should know what you are signing.

This is false. The so-called mortgage specialist should have explained how the mortgage would work. A majority of the Sub Prime loans are taken over the telephone and are worked up by the lender and mailed to you for your signature in a self-addressed envelope. Once received by the lender, if approved, the lender will order Title, if a clear Title, you are ready to close, and the appointment is set at your home. In most cases you will never see the lender, never mind talk to them again. If you live in a state that has a mortgage tax that you have to pay,

and you are dealing with out of state bankers, banks or your own state mortgage broker, unless you know enough to ask, "Why
do I have to pay the mortgage tax on the
amount I now owe, which is old money, or
get a re-issue discount on my Title?"

As I have stated at the beginning of this
story, some brokers either do not know or
will not ever tell you that you could save
thousands of dollars in closing costs. Most
out of state banks that are doing your refinancing, do not even know about a mortgage
tax, as their state does not have the tax. On
many occasions I have tried speaking with
the out of state lenders and was told that
they never heard of a mortgage tax.

Refinancing, not on a purchase can save
this tax; the old money state tax is saved
when the bank that currently has your mortgage will assign your mortgage to the new
bank. In other words, one bank has to re-
lease the mortgage and the new bank has to
accept the mortgage.

If you refinance with the same bank that
now has your mortgage, tell the same bank
that you want to save the old money, which
is the amount you now owe, without paying

the State Mortgage Tax all over again. If the bank rep does not know or does not tell you about this tax, I suggest talking to another bank rep.

Sub-Prime

There are borrowers that were given high rates and a lot of points. The broker, banker or bank said after running a credit report and checking the borrowers income, "Sorry, I can't get you the thirty year fixed rate at 6.5% that you applied for, because your credit was not good, or in the guidelines, or you did not have enough income to qualify for the A-paper Conforming Rates.

If you really want to buy the home that your family fell in love with, or you needed to refinance and do a cash-out on your residence, we can give you a mortgage anyway at a higher Sub Prime Rate, say 8 ½ % to 9 ¼ % if you really need the mortgage. Remember, you will sign almost anything, as your family needs a place to live. Or your creditors payments are getting harder and harder to pay and you are under a lot of pressure to do something before your world collapses.

You are thinking, "Boy we really need the home or, boy, I will save a couple of hundred dollars if I refinance my 6% Fixed

Rate that I now have, to an 8 ½ % to 9 ½ % new mortgage. I need the home for my family." Or, "I need to pay all the debts on my credit cards. Before I go insane with pressure, I better take the new mortgage, and then I can relieve the pressure."

You don't realize that if you take a monthly 1 to 3% mortgage, which adjusts monthly up to 17% or stick with the 8 ½ to 9 ½ % for one to three years, that it will adjust up to 16% over time, not realizing at the time what you are really getting into. Guess what? The lenders got you where they wanted to, or you are told you can get out of the mess, in three years as you now signed for a mortgage with a Pre-Penalty. This means if you try to refinance the Sub-Prime loan to a decent rate, you will have to pay 1 to 3% in pre-payment penalties back to your lender to get out of the mess you're in.

This will cost you thousands to the lender to get out, as they want to keep your mortgage or have sold your mortgage to a major investor for a huge profit. This is happening across the country. Read the newspapers and turn on the TV, you will hear about the fraud and conniving that is going on every day. If you have ever watched 'Dateline,' and Nightline thousands of Homeowners are both giving up and losing their homes due to foreclosures and Sub-Prime loans, which never should have been given to these poor homeowners.

Keep in mind, the loan specialist could care less, as the more Sub-Prime and monthly loans they give out, the more money is made from these loans. If you didn't notice, the day you closed the loan with the XYZ Lender, the loan was sold to the ABC lender. Have you noticed that you now send your mortgage payment not to XYZ, but ABC instead? Guess what? The major investors who bought the Sub-Prime loans thought the loans were a fantastic investment for their shareholders, knowing that the poor borrower will eventually have to pay up to 17% rates.

The major investors are losing billions of dollars because the loans backfired and borrowers could not pay the monthly increases on their mortgages. Now the investors have no idea what to do as they are left with foreclosed properties and homeowners are walking away because they cannot pay the increases every time the loan is adjusted. Read the newspapers and watch TV to see what is going on in this country. It is finally dawning on the Federal Government that mortgages are out of control. It is time for the State Banking Departments across the country to start investigating the fraud and the Federal Government to investigate the same.

For every mortgage application filled out across the country, on the last page of the application form 1003, it states that it is a crime to any person who may suffer any loss due to Reliance upon any misrepresentation that I have made on this application and/or criminal penalties including, but not limited to fines or imprisonment or both, under the provisions of Title 18, United States Code Sec. 1001, et seq as part of the form, which must be signed by the borrowers and the Loan Specialist taking and filling out the application.

Did the loan officer who took the application with the borrower face to face or over the telephone say, "Don't worry, I will make sure you have enough income to qualify you for the mortgage?" Or, "Don't worry, if you make $25,000 per year, I will put $65,000 on the application to qualify you."

At the closing you did not look at the form 1003 application to see if they put $25,000 or $65,000 in income, and you signed the 1003 form at closing without reviewing the form. Who is at fault? You are partly at fault and the one representing the bank is also at fault. What you did not know at closing is that one of the forms you were told to sign was called a form 4506.T This form is used by the lender to obtain your Federal Tax return from the Internal Revenue Service, if the lender feels that they need to compare your actual Tax Return to what was put on the 1003 application that you signed at closing, both forms are signed by the borrower.

I personally have both forms explained to my client at the time of the application or at closings, which I attend personally, to make sure my client knows exactly what they are signing. The forms I have mentioned are very rarely explained to the borrower. Very rarely is the form 4506 T explained to the borrower. If the loan is not closed with an attorney, once again, I stress paying an accountant or attorney to review all forms sent by the lender in the mail or before you close the loan. You will save hundreds of dollars if you are not sure about the mortgage.

The majority of income tax filers used accountants to file their taxes or hired an attorney to represent them when they purchased their homes. Call them - they will advise you on the type of mortgage you applied for, to make sure you are getting exactly what the one who took the application face to face, or especially the lender that took the information over the telephone and sent you the mortgage papers to sign: told you.

How to save your home

I suggest if you know that your mortgage payments are constantly going up and you are barely paying the increases think about what will happen to your family if you lose your home.

First: You are forced to move because your lender forecloses on you, you will have to move, probably out of the area where your children go to school.

Second: When you lose your home, you will have to rent somewhere, out of the neighborhood.

Third: It might cost just as much to rent as you are paying for your mortgage, especially if you need room for your children.

Fourth: Usually a landlord wants a credit report and references. Your credit report will show a foreclosure on the report and late payments to your creditors, normally a landlord would not take a chance and rent to you.

Fifth: It will usually cost you at least two months security, one-month rent and figure on one month for moving expenses. If your rent were $2000 per month, it would cost you $4,000 for security, $2,000 rent, and 2,000 to move, which would be $8,000. This is the cost to move out of your dream home with your family. You will have to start all over again. Do you have $8,000?

Sixth: You would lose your tax write off on mortgage interest and property taxes, because you cannot deduct rent. This would take you a few years to save for a down payment and get your credit back in good standing. How can you start saving enough to start all over again?

My advice: Hold on.

I have seen and heard of borrowers getting ripped off across the country for no other reason than pure greed, and the borrowers had no idea until it was too late what they got into, because it wasn't explained to them. I have been in this business over twenty years, both in good times and bad times, and never even dreamed of what has happened over the past few years in the mortgage business, that the business has gone to the lowest scams imaginable and put this country in such a mess with people losing their homes over pure greed.

The crime is that the State Banking Departments, State Attorney Generals, and the Federal Government let this get so far. It is completely out of hand, but it is not too late to get back on our feet. Remember you could possibly resolve the national mortgage problem by following the steps in this book and not lose your dream of owning your home.

Remember that you can beat the system at they're own game. Never go back to the lender, broker or banker who gave you the mortgage in the first place. Remember what you got involved with. Also, look at the advertisements and your mail and television. Most companies now want you to go back to them for another mortgage. Think before you act. Ask questions and get it in writing. If they are reputable, you will get exactly what you want. Remember; if you can't get a mortgage right now, try following my suggestions. Eventually you will get the mortgage. Hold on.

I would also suggest, if you think you were coerced into getting one of the mortgages that caused this National crisis, write to your State Banking Department and your State Attorney General, or even call your television News Station. They usually have an investigative department that will look into the problem for you, if you ever tell them your story.

Try your local congressman, Assemblyman, or Senator in your district, as their jobs are representing the people. If enough borrowers call, action will be taken. There is no reason why you should lose your dream of home ownership. Once again, review your Hud-1 closing statement. If you think you were overcharged in broker or banker lender points, fees, commissions or Yield Spread Premiums, call the above parties.

I can only say in summarizing this book, sometimes I look and think with all that's going on in the mortgage business today, that this crisis will eventually ease, like it has over the years. The honest mortgage professionals will still be in business, eventually the dishonest mortgage professionals will be long gone and we will have a clean, honest, industry once again.

As of right now, I have heard people not trusting the banks, bankers, brokers, etc.

anymore because of the dishonesty in the business. I feel that the only mortgage professionals that object and complain about this book are the ones who caused this crisis in the first place. Once again, I say to you homeowners, 'Hold on' and keep your dream, there is a way. Remember, eventually housing prices will increase and you will be glad you held on.

This crisis will eventually end. After spending your hard earned money and life savings to obtain your current home, if you give up now, remember that it is very hard to start all over again.

(Read the attached newspaper statements and mail I am still getting. They are now advising me to refinance to fixed rates from the same companies that offered me the 1% loans and Sub-Prime loans.)

I have been through this crisis before, let's look back at the Real Estate market. Only a few years ago, the Real Estate industry was pushing prices of homes up. There was no limit as to how high the prices could go. Mortgages were given to borrowers that really couldn't afford to buy. Now the Real Estate industry is advising homeowners to lower their prices if they want to sell. That means we are in a crisis. In the late eighties and mid nineties housing was also at a low, if you bought a home for $200,000, you could not sell it for $200,000. You would have lost your down payment, plus closing costs and sold below the original purchase price.

For those that decided to stay and not sell below the market, after a few years the same $200,000 home was worth $350,000. The current market will eventually turn around and those who held on and not panicked will see their houses once again increase in value, as rates on mortgages are currently low. Think about the consequences and discuss them with your family, as you might not get the opportunity to buy again. Hold on.

How to Survive Without Losing Your Home

As your mortgage keeps going up and you cannot refinance, because your credit does not qualify at a new fixed rate. To absorb the increase, the majority of homeowners will get a large income tax refund that they didn't expect, as you can write off your mortgage interest and also your property taxes, which are a large deduction on your schedule 'A' itemized deduction on your Federal 1040 income tax return. Also, you can deduct any points that you paid to your broker, banker or bank that were paid by you when you purchased your home.

First: Look at your Hud-1 closing statement and also the checks you wrote out at closing. If you refinanced your home and points to your broker, banker or bank from the refinanced, amount, you can deduct them, provided they were paid from the new loan amount. By dividing the points by the number of years of the loan, if you paid at closing, $3000. in points for thirty years, you can deduct one thirty per year. If you paid your broker, banker or bank out of your pocket, not from the loan, you can deduct the whole amount paid on schedule A of the 1040 Return. You cannot deduct Premium Mortgage Insurance, which is absorbed in your mortgage payments.

This figure, PMI shows on the new 2007 form 1099, which is sent by your lender, it will show PMI separately on the 1099 interest form sent by the lender. Again, check your Hud-1 closing statement to find the points. Make sure you bring this to your accountant's attention when you file the IRS Tax Refund. This will get you up to date on your mortgage if you are behind a month or two, keep the balance of the refund, if possible, to try and pay any new increases on your mortgage that will be coming, if you have one of the adjustable rate mortgages.

Second: If your adjustable rate mortgage is increasing, I suggest telling your employer that you want to add two or three dependents on your W3 Form for dependents. This will increase your paycheck and give you more take-home pay on your weekly, bi-weekly or monthly paycheck. Remember, you have a refund on your next year's taxes to absorb the dependents. Talk to your accountant, he will advise you if it's feasible to take the dependents now.

Third: If you work for a fairly large company, at the end of every year and by Quarter, they will send you a report which tells you how much you have in your pension plan and 401K Savings. This is an asset. You might think about borrowing from the plan, if it is allowed. I have had some clients of mine borrow from the plans to purchase their homes. Usually you can do this for housing, medical or educational. I suggested borrowing from the plans usually at a low interest or none at all, as part of the money you contribute is out of your paycheck. You can be charged a penalty of 10% if the loan is not borrowed. Usually you can start savings again in the plan after a year or two.

Fourth: For the homeowners who got sold on the monthly adjustable at 1 to 3% with caps up to 17%, and the homeowners who got sold on the sub-prime mortgages, I suggest obtaining your credit reports and take the report to a legitimate lender and ask to apply for what is called an FHA Loan also known as a Federal Housing Administration, secure loan, which is Government insured.

The FHA loan on a one-family home maximum mortgage is currently approximately, $362,750, which will eventually be raised to $417,000 on a one family home, as soon as the Federal Government passes it. This has already been passed by the U.S Senate and is waiting for final approval. This loan is compatible to the FNMA Conforming 'A' Paper Fixed Rate Loan without the credit criteria that you must have. For 'A' Paper Fixed Rate with credit guidelines you cannot meet.

The credit guidelines on a FHA Government insured mortgage are less strict, and you can get the FHA mortgage without the FICO Score and past and current credit problems with a written explanation, or no credit at all, providing you can show utility bills, insurance, etc, with letters that you pay your bills on time, you must show your income to qualify, bring two years of your W2's, a month of pay stubs, a letter from your employer stating your salary, your job position and length of employment, if you have changed jobs before applying for the mortgage with FHA, you will need the information from your prior employer.

The FHA mortgage rates, which are fixed, are similar to the conforming conventional rates and the FHA credit guidelines have less than perfect credit criteria. I stress that you do not go to a lender, broker, etc., who is not approved to do FHA Mortgages, as you will be charged additional points.also check for the new FHA maximum loan amounts which will increase again in the future

Over Charges To You

Be wary of over-charges. When you apply for a mortgage at application, you will be expected to pay for the appraisal, sometimes an application fee and/or processing fee, and also you might be charged for a Credit Report Fee. This must be done by the one taking the application. Do not pay more than $25.00 for the Credit Report and also ask how much the appraiser charges. It is usually, $275.00 to $350.00 for a one family home, which is average. Never pay the commissions, points or other charges at time of application, as there should not be any other charges at application.

You must get a copy of what is called a 'Good Faith Estimate' of all closing costs itemized by line. The Good Faith Estimate will show the same figures that you paid at application, plus any points, origination fees, broker fees, and what is called a Yield Spread Premium, which is paid to the brokers, bankers, etc. by the lender they are going through.

Always ask how much you will be paying

to get the loan from the broker, banker, etc, remember, the bank usually pays them to submit the loan. If you think you are being charged over two points, question why. Remember the lender usually pays the broker, banker, etc, a yield spread premium. Question how much and why you still have to pay a broker, banker, etc. points, if they are getting a yield-spread premium from the lender.

Always ask for a copy of the Good Faith Estimate with all charges, and always ask the broker, banker or bank that you go to for a fee agreement signed by both you and the lender, showing how many points, Yield Spread Premiums, etc, you are being charged. When you go to your closing, bring the agreement with you in case you are being overcharged. If you don't question the fees, in some cases you will be charged more.

Before signing the Hud-1 at your closing, review the fees, commissions, etc. and question the Hud-1. If you think the charges are more than you agreed to when you did the application, or if the bank you are dealing with wants to close at their bank attorney's office, the bank attorney will go over the fees with you to make sure you are not being overcharged. If you feel more comfortable, bring your attorney to the closing and let them look over the charges on the Hud-1 closing statement.

On your refinancing, remember you have what is called a 'Three-Day Right of Recession' by law to cancel the mortgage, which the bank attorney will explain to you at closing. If a lender tells you that they will close at your home, beware. It is up to you to question the Hud-1 closing statement with questioned charges. I suggest bringing your accountant or attorney to the closing to question any charges that they think are excessive.

I have heard horror stories of borrowers being charged up to 10 points at closings, after the borrowers closed. I have seen the Hud-1s with their predatory fees that were charged and not known to the borrowers. It is a shame that the borrowers signed for the loans and were told at the beginning that their closing costs were $7,000. Then at the closing, they were $18,000, without the borrower knowing why. The borrowers just wanted to get the closing over with and were too embarrassed to question why the closing cost changed so much all of a sudden.

When applying for your loan, if you are told that you don't have enough income to obtain the amount of the mortgage, and you are told, "Don't worry, the loan officer will put down enough income to qualify you or add something extra on your income or show a job that you don't have," you will be signing the Form 1003 which is the mortgage application and you will also have to sign the form 4506 - T, stating this is your true income which might go to the Internal Revenue Service for verification of income reported. Which is sent by the lender you have committed a fraud. The Form 4506 – T, could be given to you at closing instead of at application. Always review your 1003 Loan Application which you were told to sign at time of closing.

Again, I must stress, when you apply for a refinance, insist on a copy of your rate Lock-In and Fee Agreement. Showing points commissions and yield spread premiums paid by the bank to the mortgage broker, mortgage banker or if going directly to a bank a copy of all charges, if you think you are being over charged do not deal with the broker, banker or bank.

Always remember, before you think about purchasing or refinancing, bring your credit report with you at time of application, along with all of your income verification and bank statements, 401K, pension and/or saving plans currently received by your employer. This information will be reviewed by the lender to get you approved for the best rate available at the time of application. Also, ask the broker, banker or bank what are the charges, points, yield spread premiums, commissions, etc. to obtain the loan. Remember, you want this agreement in writing; also, if you lock in your rate for 30, 45, or 60 days you want a written verification from the lender of the lock in rate. If you take a loan from a lender over the telephone, which I don't recommend, always keep a copy of the documents sent by the lender, as they will want to close the loan at your home. Compare your copies of the documents to the loan documents prepared by the lender before signing, same procedure at closing.

It's amazing that one of the lenders who wrote and sold the majority of the sub prime and one percent and above mortgages, is now selling their bank before going into bankruptcy to another bank and receiving over 100 million dollars and walking away leaving this mortgage mess behind and to hell with the poor borrowers. Why have they not been investigated for fraud?

If all resources fail, try calling your bank and ask for a modification on your mortgage. As banks are not in the real estate business and will try and work out a solution with you to save your home as the last thing a bank wants is to foreclose and hold real estate. There are solutions if you sit down, think about and discuss the problem. Remember this mortgage and real estate crisis will eventually end.

Review the six steps on pages 39 and 40 and also remember when you bought your home, you paid closing costs in the thousands of dollars and your down payment whether it was 3%, 5%, 10% or 20% down to purchase your home, do you want to lose everything? Why would you purchase your dream, and just walk away after losing thousands of dollars? Remember what you had to do to come up with the closing costs and down payment and try to start all over again. Remember your house will eventually go up in value and you will be glad that you held on to your dream. Remember my advice on page 40, home values will go up and you will be glad that you took the advice in my book.

I know that many financial experts will disagree with me but, I do still suggest borrowing from pensions and or 401K plans. As the loan is paid back out of your paycheck eventually you will get an increase (raise) in your paycheck to make up the loan deduction, which is automatically taken out, this will keep you from not losing your home, as most loans borrowed are short term and you are still invested in them. Once the loan is paid back, you can start again for your retirement. As the crisis is now, not in ten to twenty years, also remember that most pension and 401K plans are losing your money due to bad investments and the economy. Remember that down the road the home you bought for $350,000.00 will eventually be worth over $500,000.00 in a few years from now. Think about the present, not about the future. What is more important to you and your family? A comfortable place to live with your family now as you still have time to save for your future. Remember you will not only lose your home and have to save all over again, but, also lose your tax right off and the equity you put into your home and the equity you will make in the future if you hold on, *Don't Lose Your Dream.*

Beware Of The Old Scam...
Still In Town Now More Than Ever

Homeowner's in default with their mortgage lenders are now being contacted by investors looking to rescue the homeowners with a new scam. They are told to sign over their title of the house and that they can stay in their home as renters, in the belief that they can eventually buy back their home at a later date. This is a complete scam, as soon as the title is transferred, the home is usually refinanced to obtain as much cash as possible, and when payments are not made on the new mortgage with the new owner therefore, the house again goes into foreclosure. The scam artist usually will offer the original homeowner a few thousand dollars to transfer the title over to the scam artist, with a promise that the original homeowner can rent their own house and buy it back at a later date. This will never happen, as you now do not own your home, the scam artist will try to sell the home you once owned to what is called a straw buyer, and make as much profit as possible on the home you once owned, leaving you out in the street.

You have now lost everything, and have to find another place to live. The scam artist could care less, if you lose your home and are evicted and put out of your house. Never, ever, sign over your title until you have spoken to your attorney and the bank that currently holds your mortgage. The scam artist has public access to all of your information this is how you are contacted by them. Beware the scam artist will find a straw buyer which is a borrower willing to try and refinance the same home that was transferred to him on title or sell the house whichever makes him the most money usually before the home goes into foreclosure, as the straw buyer will never make a mortgage payment on the original home. *Beware In this wonderful country Americans are well known to fight for what is theirs and their families I know we can beat the system if you only think about the consequences involved hold on and don't lose your dream GOD BLESS AND GOOD LUCK*